HABIT-BUSTING

HABIT-BUSTING

Boost your self-esteem

PETE COHEN

**Foreword by Eve Cameron,
Editor of *She* Magazine**

Element
An Imprint of HarperCollins*Publishers*
77–85 Fulham Palace Road
Hammersmith, London W6 8JB

The website address is:
www.thorsonselement.com

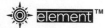 element™

and *Element* are trademarks of
HarperCollins*Publishers* Limited

Published by Element 2003

10 9 8 7 6 5 4 3 2 1

A catalogue record of this book
is available from the British Library

ISBN 0 00 715497 6

Printed and bound in Great Britain by
Martins The Printers Limited, Berwick upon Tweed

Contents

Foreword

I first met Pete Cohen when we were filming a television series a few years ago. Watching him in action reminded me of those American TV evangelists who hold their audiences in their thrall, move them to tears, make them laugh and inspire them absolutely. Over time, I've seen Pete help people to change their lives in lots of different ways, including through conquering their phobias, losing weight and getting fitter, building their self-esteem and through managing their relationships more effectively. On a personal level, Pete has helped me enormously with work and confidence issues.

The best news is that all those tips, ideas, techniques and exercises that Pete shared with me and all those others who've changed their lives are here in this book to help you get to where you want to be. It's a sort of 'pocket Pete'. But of course, just as joining a gym isn't actually a guarantee of getting fit (you have to go and work hard to see results!), reading a self-help book won't sort your life out – only you can do that. I think a really good place to start is with one of my favourite Pete questions, which you'll find in this book. It's about imagining yourself aged 90 and asking yourself "What do I wish I'd done less of in my life?" Next you ask "What do I wish I'd done more of?" Enjoy exploring your answers!

Eve Cameron
Editor
She Magazine

Introduction

My name is Pete Cohen and I have been helping people bust their habits for over 10 years.

I have always found human behaviour fascinating, and through my explorations and experiences of working with thousands of people I have become convinced that the majority of people can overcome their limiting habits. Habits are quite simply things we have learned. They are thoughts, behaviours and actions that we have practised over time.

No one was born with low self-esteem, no one was born with an eating disorder, no one was born biting their nails or with a tendency to procrastinate. All habits are behaviours we have learned and practised so often that they have become *second* nature. And because they are part of our second nature, and not our first, we are closer to our true selves without them. We only feel they are part of us because we have practised them for so long and are conditioned to have them. We often end up feeling that they are who we are. They are not.

The habit-busting techniques and exercises in this book will help you to unlearn your habit of low self-esteem and replace it with more productive and enjoyable ways of living your life. You will learn how to make simple but highly effective changes, and ultimately you will gain more confidence and control and become freer and happier.

Low self-esteem is a habit, a behaviour that you have learned and practised so often that it has become second nature. You have hardwired your brain to believe that you are not good enough. But it doesn't have to be this way.

What Causes Low Self-esteem?

Where does it come from, this low self-esteem?

When we were babies we were happy. We were content with ourselves; self-esteem and confidence were just words. We learnt to talk because we needed to communicate to others when we wanted things. As we learnt to communicate, we were subjected to the world: family values, culture, religion, education and government. We learnt to judge ourselves by those values, many people to the point of thinking that there was something wrong with them.

Young children are happy with who they are. But as we get older, many of us are no longer happy with ourselves. We are living our lives by other people's ideals and values, and the rules that have been given to us. Did we have any say in the values that have been given to us? No.

Most people choose to accept the status quo. We accept the expectations that have been handed down to us, some of which have been given to us by our parents or our families. But when are you going to stop being your parents' you? Or your husband's you? When are you going to choose simply to be yourself? Expectations tend to lead to a chronic sense that we are not good enough. We are left with a permanent sense of failure. Many of us have a feeling inside that we are not good enough the way that we are. And when we have that sense, the way that we move through the world, the way we think, the way that we act, everything, will reflect what goes on inside.

But this feeling of worthlessness is just an illusion. It *is* possible for you to have high self-esteem – to feel confident and worthy, and in control of your life – and it is easy to achieve it. Boosting your self-esteem is simply a matter of personal choice: of choosing to have your *own* values, of choosing to judge yourself by those values, and of choosing to believe in your own self-worth.

You have been acting the part of someone who has low self-esteem. As I mentioned earlier, you weren't born that way; it is a behaviour that you have learnt and practised over time, and you are good at it. In fact, this is your biggest challenge: you are so good at feeling bad about yourself and giving yourself a hard time, it has actually become your comfort zone! Many people who have low self-esteem are comfortable with it, and with this feeling of comfort comes a kind of security. This is why many people try at all costs to avoid change. The question you need to ask yourself is: *Am I prepared to change?* Because the only way you are going to change is by moving outside of your comfort zone – and to do this, you need to start taking care of yourself and enjoying your life.

This book will offer simple but highly effective strategies to help you change into the person you want to be and stop the self-destructive processes of low self-esteem. Because low esteem is very simple – it basically revolves around the things that you internalize: how you communicate with yourself and the pictures that you make in your mind. Most of us don't even realize that we talk to ourselves all the time. And the way you live your life and the quality of your self-esteem comes down to that very simple thing: how do you communicate with yourself?

For years you might have lived as your parents' you, your friends' you, your teachers' you, your partner's you and your bosses' you, but where on earth are YOU.

ROBERT HARPER

Stop Putting Yourself Down

I believe the basic quality of our lives is defined by how well or how badly we treat ourselves and communicate with ourselves. We are always asking ourselves questions, talking to ourselves and giving ourselves messages. The conclusions and answers we draw from these conversations help us to reach decisions about the way we live our lives. The problem is, most people ask themselves the wrong questions, such as '*Why* didn't it work?' or '*Why* can't I do that?', or '*Why* did they say that?'

When trying to break the habit of low self-esteem, we more often than not ask ourselves '*Why* can't I stop giving myself a hard time/putting myself down?' The brain will only ever try to offer a helpful answer – there are always endless reasons why we can't do something! But to get from it a far more effective and useful answer we need to learn to explore our own potential to help ourselves by asking '*What* could I be doing to gain control and improve my self-esteem?' What you think about is what you tend to get. You set the direction you want to take.

Most people are used to and therefore very good at giving themselves a hard time. Are you? Consider for a moment whether you would treat your best friend the way you treat yourself. Giving ourselves a hard time is probably one of the most common habits of those who live in the Western world, yet none of us was born with this habit. We learn how to analyze and criticize ourselves from others as we grow up.

It is said that one of the first signs of madness is talking to ourselves. If this were true, we must all be mad, because we all do it, all the time. The reason it mostly goes unnoticed, even by ourselves, is that we do it inside our heads. We say to ourselves 'I am stupid', or 'I can't do anything properly', or 'Nobody likes me'.

Having such thoughts, for many of us, is like eating: we do it automatically, without really appreciating what is going into our bodies (or our minds). What often gets forgotten is that these thoughts, in many ways like the kinds of food we eat, shape our lives. It is helpful to take a really close look at our thoughts and change them to develop a more positive attitude.

Keep A Record

Get a diary or a notebook and write down how you feel about yourself. If you have low self-esteem, you will be very judgmental and critical of yourself. I want you to step back from yourself and observe. All you need to do with your information to begin with is to record it. Don't analyze it. Just write it down. Becoming more aware of what you say to yourself and how you treat yourself is the key to change.

You need to gather information before you can master your state of mind. Humans have, on average, between 50,000 and 60,000 thoughts a day. That's a lot of thoughts! So what do people think about? Most people think old thoughts: they think about what they thought about yesterday. They focus on what's wrong with and what's missing from their lives, and then they fail to change. Because, in life, you get what you focus on. We victimize ourselves with the way that we talk to ourselves.

Keep a record of all your thoughts and the sorts of things you say to yourself. Would you treat anyone else the way you treat yourself? Knowing your thoughts is the first step. Once you understand what you are doing to yourself, you can begin to challenge these thoughts. For example, you can say to yourself 'I *am* good enough', or 'I *am* as attractive as I need to be'. Be aware that if you feel insecure or ignored it is up to you to change that. Don't rely on other people to tell you that you have done a good job, because they won't always be there for you. But you can tell *yourself* you are good enough. Be prepared to pat yourself on the back.

Create Your Own Inner Coach

A friend of mine once worked with a famous French football player. One day he asked him, 'Do you ever give yourself a hard time?' The player, who did not speak great English, looked a little confused, so my friend asked whether he ever talked to himself inside his head when he made a mistake. The puzzled look on the player's face cleared as he retorted, 'Ahhh, you mean zee duck in my head!'

It was now my friend's turn to be confused, until he realized what the Frenchman was really saying. 'Yes,' my friend replied, 'that's right, the duck!'

Now, not everyone has a duck in their head, but everyone talks to themselves.

My friend then asked this player, 'Have you ever thought about telling the duck to shut up?' This question made him laugh initially, but it made him realize that he could soften this voice so that it was not critical and judgmental.

And this is something you need to remember when you are tackling your low self-esteem: you are in control of your inner voice and you can alter what it says accordingly. The quality of our lives comes down to how well we communicate with ourselves. If we are gentle and kind to ourselves we feel good about ourselves, and the opposite is true if we are hard on ourselves.

Do you remember when you were a child? Did you have an imaginary friend or pet, or did you ever imagine that you were a doctor or a nurse or a fireman? I want you to use that same imagination to create your own Inner Coach.

I always encourage people who want to improve their self-esteem to do this – to create a made-up coach inside their heads, whose job is to keep them focused on breaking their habit of being hard on themselves.

Your Inner Coach will be responsible for managing your state of mind and it will help you to look at the things you say to yourself. Get a notebook to help you create and design your Inner Coach.

Consider the Following

What sort of voice would you like your Inner Coach to have? It could be like a motivational speaker's voice that inspires and keeps you positive. It could be soft and gentle, keeping you calm and relaxed. Or perhaps it could be seductive and sexy like Barry White!

Play around with your Inner Coach and give it time to operate in the way that works best for you. Be patient, as the idea of taking care of yourself in this way might seem a little strange at first.

Your Inner Coach's Responsibilities

1. To be positive.
2. To be encouraging at all times and to stamp out any worries or concerns.
3. To be gentle and kind to you – not criticizing you, judging you or giving you a hard time.
4. To keep you focused on your outcome – for you to be in control and relaxed, having busted your habit of low self-esteem for good.
5. To keep you on track, and to help you with some of the exercises that will follow in this book.
6. To remind you in a way that is instantaneous and powerful of your desire to feel good about yourself if you are 'triggered' to feel negative for any reason.
7. To always put things back into perspective with reassuring words.
8. To get you to relax and keep a positive perspective by reminding you to breathe deeply and slowly.
9. To use the mantra of **'Shut the Duck Up'** to cancel out any doubting voices you might have in your head.
10. To remind you to celebrate every day that you are getting stronger.
11. To help you by suggesting alternative thoughts that make you feel good.

12. To deal with setbacks and possible lapses in a construc-
tive and forward-thinking manner.

As you create and design your Inner Coach, you might like to
think what sort of things you would you say to yourself if you
were more confident. If you caught sight of your reflection in the
mirror and you said to yourself that you were not good enough,
how would your Inner Coach help you?

With the guidance of your Inner Coach, pay more attention to
your internal dialogue and become more aware of what you say
to yourself and how you treat yourself. If you find you are talking
to yourself in a negative or derogatory manner, tell yourself to
'Shut the Duck Up', then give yourself some encouragement
and be kind, as you would be to a child or a best friend.

Be Open to Change

As I mentioned earlier, many people find change uncomfortable, even if they have a strong desire to do so. We are all very
much creatures of comfort. You may feel bad about yourself for
many different reasons, all of which become a habit over time.
Our brains go to great lengths to try and protect us from making

changes, as they think what we have been doing is what we are supposed to do.

The following exercise is called 'Thumbs' and it demonstrates how we instinctively regard change as uncomfortable.

1. Interlock your fingers, with one thumb sitting on top of the other thumb. Notice how that feels – it should feel pretty normal and comfortable.
2. Now unlock your hands and put them back together so that the other thumb is on top. How does that feel? The chances are that it feels distinctly uncomfortable, as though the wrong thumb is on top.
3. Now go back to the other, comfortable way – aaah, that probably feels better, as if this is how it is meant to be.
4. Now interlock your fingers once again, with one thumb sitting on top of the other. Now switch the position of your thumbs back and forth at least 21 times, and, as strange as this may seem, say, either in your head or out loud, 'I LOVE TO CHANGE!'
5. After 21 times, stop and notice how it feels when you swap the position of your thumbs around. It will start to feel more comfortable.

This is a physical illustration of how the brain naturally directs us to what it thinks is most comfortable and what we have done before. This might sound strange when applied to your low self-esteem because you might not think that there is anything comfortable about you continuing to feel bad about yourself. However, it is possible that feeling good about yourself is more uncomfortable than feeling bad. This is why the easiest course of action is to keep doing what you have done before. Your low self-esteem is quite simply something you have practised, and whenever we try something that we don't normally do our brains complain – 'It's not me, it's not the way I do things.'

All I am going to be asking you to do to boost your self-esteem is to change the way you do things. By doing the simple exercises and techniques in this book, and practising them over time, you will be able to feel good about yourself – permanently.

In order to change a habit, you need to re-programme your brain. Do you want to victimize yourself for the rest of your life? Instead of feeling bad about yourself because that is what you always do, would you like to learn how to take control, and be more responsible for your life, and learn how to focus your attention on more liberating ways of behaving?

It is important to embrace change because it is the only constant. If you are resistant to change you are going to struggle, whichever way you look at it. On the other hand, if you are open to change, and open to the possibility that you don't have to have low self-esteem, you can replace it with something else.

The good news is that right now, you CAN change. I have seen people do it. I have watched people become more positive about themselves and build up their self-esteem, and generally enjoy life more.

Before I go on, please remember these three absolute truths.

1. **Every human being has positive worth.** That worth is non-negotiable. Your worth is always there, and it's always going to be there, in spite of the low self-esteem you may have developed during your life. Nothing that happens in life can change that.

2. **Other people's reactions to what you do and say are just that – other people's reactions.** Their reactions, comments and attitudes are theirs, not yours. The only person who can define you is you. You are not responsible for how other people feel about you.

3. **Every person has within them all of the strengths and resources necessary to change into the person they want to be.**

Winning starts with beginning.

ROBERT SCHULLER

About This Book

This book contains a simple step-by-step strategy to help you raise your self-esteem and boost your confidence levels. With its habit-busting techniques and exercises, it gives you all the tools necessary to tackle the stubborn, self-sabotaging behaviour that is preventing you from being the person you want to be, and to put in place productive patterns that will lead to a happier, healthier and more fulfilling future.

It is important to remember, however, that it is not the techniques themselves which are going to help you change, but what you *do* with them. It is only through repetition, through practising and applying the techniques, that you will get results. Repetitive practice makes perfect practice, so do the exercises I give you with conviction, determination and desire, and be committed.

I do not want you to do one exercise straight after another. There is no rush. The exercises will be more effective if you take a break between them. Please give yourself time to change; you have worked hard at creating your low self-esteem and need the time you deserve to bring about change. **You should give yourself at least 21 days to work through the exercises.** It may seem like a long time – but it is not that long when you think that you have been putting yourself down for a lifetime!

As well as encouraging you to take breaks, I have also inserted between some of the main exercises smaller, occasionally more physical exercises to add a bit more fun to the process and also to break up what can be a fairly intense experience.

⊘ Whenever you do any of the exercises, try to ensure you are as free as possible from distractions.

⊘ Always have a notebook and pen handy.

⊘ When preparing to do an exercise, remember that if you want things to look up, you will have to start doing so. Your head must be up and your eyes on the horizon when beginning an exercise, because when you look down you start talking negatively to yourself.

Are you ready to change into the person you've always wanted to be? If so, read on.

One of the most important results you can bring into the world is the you that you really want to be.

ROBERT FRITZ

Make a Firm Commitment to Change

What precedes all behaviours, actions and performances? What turns a dream into a reality? The answer is *choices*. Your choices determine what you think, how you feel, what you do and whom you become.

It is often your choices, and not your conditions, that hold you back. If you choose to boost your self-esteem, and commit to making some different choices to the ones you are making now, you will succeed.

How come some people have high self-esteem while others don't? It is because they make different choices. They commit to achieving, and do whatever it takes to succeed.

That is why I want you not only to make a real decision to change, but also to make a contract with yourself. Don't worry, it is not legally binding – but it will help to get you focused and committed to breaking your habit of low self-esteem. It is your actions, remember, that will generate success.

Make a firm commitment to boost your self-esteem, because this commitment will unlock the energy to achieve it.

Contract

I will do the exercises in this book regularly and with determination, and add to my daily life those that work best for me.
I will honour my decision to boost my self-esteem and become a happier and healthier person.
I can and will succeed.

Signed: _____

Dated: _____

To change one's life: start immediately. Do it flamboyantly. No exceptions, no excuses.

WILLIAM JAMES

Practise Using Your Imagination

step 2

I've already mentioned the importance of making choices, because it is your choices that unlock the action necessary to break a habit. The main tool that is going to help you is learning how to use your mind in more powerful and productive ways. And the first step in doing this is learning how to use your imagination.

Everyone uses their imagination all the time, but not necessarily in particularly effective or productive ways.

If I were to ask you:

⊘ What did you have for dinner last night?
⊘ Where was your last holiday?
⊘ What colour is an orange?
⊘ What does your best friend look like?

You'd immediately make a picture of them.

Using your imagination in this way is also known as 'visualization'. I prefer to call it *effective thinking*. Visualization is not a technique – as I have shown, you already do it every day. It is how human beings process information about their world. The difference is how you *use* this in-built skill.

Some people are naturally more visual than others, but we can all learn to visualize effectively. Visualization only becomes a technique when we put it to particular use.

In one research experiment, three groups of basketball players were prepared for practise. The first group was allowed on to the court to practise with a ball, the second group was allowed on to the court but were told just to imagine themselves playing there, while the third group was left in a room to imagine themselves playing. Each group was told to try to get the ball into the basket as many times as possible. Once each group had had time to practise in their respective ways, all were allowed on to the court to see which would score the most points. The first group were not very much improved over their normal performance, as they'd in effect been practising missing as well as scoring. The second group had improved but, being on the court, had also imagined themselves missing. It was the third group, all of whom, in the seclusion of a room away from the court, had imagined themselves scoring every time, which got the ball through the hoop most often.

The things we think about and imagine have a profound effect on how we feel. Thinking about or imagining how you will be once you have broken your self-destructive habits gives your brain a description of where you want it to take you. Doing this should also make you feel good, and because making you feel good is one of the brain's primary functions, the thought or imagining becomes a way of behaving that the brain wishes to adopt.

When you commit yourself mentally to changing your habit of putting yourself down, and start practising having made that change, the change will happen. You could just as easily decide not to, but those who really want to change will work at it repeatedly until they get the desired result.

Some people say they have trouble using their imagination in this way. A little practise is always useful, as we will be using visualization quite a lot in the exercises that follow.

Visualization is just a fancy word for remembering what something looked like, or imagining what something might look like. You have been doing it all day, every day, all your life.

There is little sense in attempting to change external conditions, you must first change your inner beliefs, then outer conditions will change accordingly.

BRIAN ADAMS, *HOW TO SUCCEED*

Exercise – Practising Visualization

1. Picture an orange.
2. See the orange getting bigger and bigger and bigger until it is the size of a football.
3. Now imagine the orange turns purple, and yellow spots appear all over it.
4. The spots light up and start flashing like the coloured lights at a disco.
5. Now imagine the spots disappear, and in their place is a cheeky, smiley face.
6. The face starts laughing and you can see two rows of beautiful pearly white teeth.
7. Imagine the orange laughing so hard that tears start squirting from the eyes.
8. The orange stops laughing now, and slowly the face disappears.
9. The orange starts to shrink until it is the size of a ping-pong ball.
10. Imagine that it starts bouncing up and down, higher and higher, until the force of the impact on the ground makes it break.
11. Splattered orange lies all over the floor.
12. Now the bits start to shrivel and shrink until they vanish.

1. See a picture of yourself feeling confident on a television screen.
2. Notice the look on your face and what you are wearing.
3. The screen gets bigger and bigger and moves towards you until you can step into it.
4. Now step into it.
5. How does it feel to wear the clothes of the confident you?
6. How does it feel to be in that state of mind?
7. Register and remember that feeling.

Using All Your Senses

To use our imaginations effectively, we need to add in the emotional and mental responses we attach to certain experiences. For when we see or visualize what we want, it is not merely in picture form, but should actually be a full sensory experience. To use your imagination dramatically – you must be able to feel, hear, smell and taste as well as see the new you. It must be as if you are there.

Here's another preparatory exercise for you to try.

Exercise – Creating a Full Sensory Experience

1. Sit comfortably, free from distraction, keeping your eyes open or closed, whichever suits you.
2. Remember the best holiday you have ever had.
3. Recall some of the things you saw or heard on this holiday, the things you smelled and tasted, and some of the things you felt.
4. Imagine being back on that holiday now.
5. Make it more real and more colourful even than you remember it.
6. Now take a couple of deep breaths. Feeling good, slowly open your eyes.
7. Take a short break, then close your eyes again (if you wish).
8. Now imagine being on a make-believe holiday.
9. Imagine you are on a beautiful beach with white sand and clear blue water.
10. You can hear the gentle sound of the waves and the seagulls calling out high in the sky.
11. You can smell the sea air and almost taste the salt.
12. You feel warm, peaceful and relaxed.
13. Take a deep breath and open your eyes.

Although you know the difference, your brain cannot distinguish between the real and the imagined holiday. The more you think about the one you made up, the more your brain starts to think that it is real. Because the nervous system cannot distinguish between a real and an imagined experience, if practised enough, the thoughts we have become a plan of what we are going to do. And the more clearly thought-out and distinctive our desire, the more passionately we will pursue it.

One of the keys to breaking a habit of low self-esteem is to imagine yourself in the future, free from your habit, doing things differently and being in control. You get what you focus on.

Mini Exercise – Making Pictures in Your Mind

From now on, become more aware of how you use your mind to visualize. When you are reading or when someone is telling you a story, think about the pictures you automatically conjure up in your head. As soon as you are able to, go and find a children's book, preferably one without pictures, and just read a couple of pages. Be aware of the pictures you make in your mind.

Imagination is more important than knowledge.

ALBERT EINSTEIN

Get into a Habit-busting State

This next step in our strategy to build self-esteem is a very important one. This is all to do with your state of mind, so I want to show you how to get into the best state to be successful whenever you do any of the exercises that follow. Believe it or not, feeling relaxed and comfortable is one of the most effective states to be in, and one of the easiest ways to get into this state is to breathe deeply.

The Importance of Breath

Oxygen is the foundation of life; without it we die. Many of us breathe through our mouths, which does not properly filter the carbon dioxide. Many emotions such as stress, anxiety, worry and fear are made worse by incorrect breathing.

You may well think you have had a lifetime's worth of practice in breathing, but as anyone who has either theatrical or medical training will tell you, the more easily you allow air in and out of your body, the easier it will be for your brain and body to function.

Slow, deep breathing is one of the most natural and immediate ways to get into a relaxed state. When people are anxious or stressed, their breathing tends to be short and shallow and into the chest, rather than deep and incorporating the whole diaphragm. It may come as a surprise to you, but making a simple, subtle change to the way you breathe can have a profound impact on your state.

Exercise – Breathe Deeply

- Stop for a minute, now.
- Sit comfortably.
- Take three deep breaths.
- Allow the second and third breath to be deeper than those before.
- Just notice what happens.

Now, let's go one step further.

- Go and get a pen, right now, and make a mark two inches below your belly button and another four inches above.
- Now take another three or four slow, deep breaths, but this time filling up this area you have marked with air. Breathe in as much air as you can comfortably manage, and slowly breathe out.
- Breathing in this way helps you to relax as you are filling the lower part of your lungs with air and allowing more oxygen into your body.

Getting into State

When someone does a sport, they need to warm up their body first to get it ready and focused for the challenge to come. Your brain is like a muscle – it needs to be warmed up before it starts to work. In most of the exercises that follow I will be asking you to do the following exercise first to get your brain warmed up and ready. This quick and simple exercise will help you to feel relaxed, yet in control, and will get you into the right state of mind for change. An icon representing this warm-up exercise (*) will appear before most other exercises, to remind you to do this one first.

Exercise – Getting into the Right State for Change *

1. Sit comfortably, focusing your attention back on your breathing so you are breathing between the two marks on your abdomen I asked you to make earlier.
2. Focus on the difference between an in-breath and an out-breath, as you allow your breathing rate to become slower and deeper.
3. Imagine you are breathing in feelings of relaxation and breathing out any tension or discomfort. As you breathe in now, imagine your breath travelling from your nose down to your toes, and as you breathe out imagine your discomfort disappearing through the soles of your feet.
4. The feeling you have now is the ideal state for change. You are likely to feel more positive and open to the possibility of change. You may feel calm, expectant, interested, alert, ready to go, excited.
5. Choose a specific word to describe how you feel at this moment – and practise letting this word drift effortlessly from your lips as you breathe out.

The more you do this exercise, the more you will feel the way you want to feel. And the better you feel, the more control you will have. You probably breathe about 25,000 or more times a day, so I challenge you to breathe that little bit more deeply. Make a habit of breathing in this way as often as you can – how about 100 times today for starters?

Mini Exercise – Relaxing Yourself from Head to Toe
To feel generally more relaxed, practise breathing slowly, in through your nose and out through your mouth. Take long, slow, comfortable breaths. Try counting backwards from 1,000 and, as you do so, relax every muscle in your body, starting from the top of your head and working down to your feet. Doing this once or twice a day will soon start to make a real difference to how you feel.

The thinking that got you into this is not going to be the thinking that gets you out of it.

MICHAEL BREEN

Choose Your Words Carefully

What words do you use to describe your intention to raise your self-esteem?

Many people do not realize that the words they use about their intention can radically affect how they feel about changing their lives. How many of us do the things we *should* do, and how many the things we *want* to?

Think about your own low self-esteem and say to yourself, for example, 'I should feel good about myself'. Notice how it feels when you say this.

Now repeat this sentence, using each of the words in the list below.

I ought to
I must
I have to

I'll try to
I hope to
I could
I may
I might
I aim to

When you use words such as 'have to', 'need to' and 'must' they make you feel as though you are putting some unnecessary pressure on yourself. Words such as 'might', 'may' and 'could' are very indecisive and are unlikely to inspire you to really go for it. When people use these words it doesn't give them a sense of conviction. They don't enthuse about their intention, because words really do affect how we think, feel and act.

Now repeat this sentence, 'I _____ feel good about myself', using each of the words in the list on page 44. Notice which one makes you feel most motivated to change. I am not asking you to find which words make you believe you can change, just which feel best for you.

I challenge you, with the words you choose, to say this personalized sentence over and over to yourself, as if you really mean it, whether or not you believe it right now.

Every time we say 'I must do something' it takes an incredible amount of energy. Far more than physically doing it.

GITA BELLIN

I will

I am going to

I can

I want to

I expect to

Now, when you use these kinds of phrases ('I am a positive person', 'I want to be in control', 'I can have high self-confidence'), what do you picture? Think about what you want to achieve, not what you want to leave behind. See yourself as being already there.

The words you choose must, when you say them to yourself, make you feel as though you are actually going to live them. If they don't, it is unlikely they will be of much help, because breaking a habit is all about changing your feelings towards it, and yourself.

The words you use must, when you say them to yourself, make you feel motivated to change.

Thinking About What You Want

Instead of thinking about what they would like to happen, most people think about what they do not want to happen by picturing things going wrong.

You say you want to change and have read this far. Maybe you do want change. Are you ready to use your imagination now to help you focus on what you would like to happen? Write down what you want to achieve.

I want _____

_____

If in the space above you have written 'to stop feeling so worthless', what immediately comes to mind? In order not to think about something, you need first to think about it. The effect of this is to leave you focused on what you don't want. The picture that comes to mind as you write out your description is of you feeling bad about yourself. You need to use a different approach.

Instead, write down in the slot what you want to achieve, for example, 'to be a positive person', 'to be relaxed, confident and happy', 'to be able to get along better with people', 'to be more self-reliant'. You will be creating a representation of something that you want your brain to find more evidence to support. This is what really can set you free from your habit.

Think about what you want to achieve, not what you want to leave behind. See yourself as being there already.

However many holy words you read, however many you speak, what good will they do you if you do not act upon them?

THE DHAMMAPADA

See Yourself How You Want to Be

If you want to break a habit of low self-esteem, you need to be able to see yourself how you want to be. In other words, you need to be able to see yourself as already having high self-esteem. You need to pretend, to imagine how you would be living your life as a confident, self-assured person, and how you might like to react in different sets of circumstances. The more you can use your imagination to help you in this, the more successful you are likely to be, because by imagining yourself as vividly as possible as this ex-habit person, you are allowing your body to prepare for the end result.

Exercise – Imagining the New You

- ⊘ Think of the new you without your low self-esteem.
- ⊘ What would the world look like through their eyes?
- ⊘ What would it be like to wear their clothes?
- ⊘ How would they stand, walk or sit?
- ⊘ How would they say 'no' and mean it?

The Future You

If you want to change, you must be able to see yourself having made that change or you will have little chance of ever achieving it.

Exercise – Stepping into the Future

1. Do the exercise that gets you into a relaxed and controlled state (*, page 37).
2. Stand up, close your eyes and imagine that your front door is before you, life-size, and behind the door is the future you without low self-esteem.

3. The door opens and you can see the back of yourself, in the future, feeling confident and self-assured.

4. Notice the difference in what you are wearing and how you feel.

5. Now the you in the future is going to turn to the side so you can see them in profile.

6. Then they move to face you. They look vibrant, amazing and full of life.

7. See the future you as clearly as you like. Move them around so you can get a really good look.

8. Now imagine stepping into the future you and feeling how it is to have high self-esteem.

9. Now do it again; step into the future you and intensify that feeling.

10. Feel the change in every cell of your body, your organs and your bones.

11. Now, physically take a step forward, into the future you.

12. Feel how it feels, see through those eyes and hear through those ears, life without low self-esteem.

13. Once you have finished, take a few deep breaths and have a break.

When you are ready do the exercise again, this time imagine you've been practising it for years. *Practise this exercise every day.*

If you want to change, you must be able to see yourself having made that change before that change can take place.

Things do not change:

we change.

HENRY DAVID THOREAU

Set Specific Goals

What is goal-setting? I believe it is getting what you want. As should be clear by now, your brain can only follow the instructions you give it. To over-ride your habit of low self-esteem, you need to give the brain a new set of well thought-out and quite specific instructions, over and over again. The instructions, or new goal(s), need to be so attractive that your brain wants to leave behind your self-destructive behaviour and move towards the new you.

In order to get what you want, you need to KNOW what you want. You must be as clear as you can be about what it is you want to achieve.

Do you have a clear idea of your own direction?

You've got to think about 'big things' while you are doing small things, so that the small things go in the right direction.

ALVIN TOFFLER

To over-ride your habit, you need to give the brain a new set of specific instructions, over and over again.

Exercise – Setting Goals

Get your notebook.
Get into state*.

1. Have your list of what you want to achieve in front of you. Is it specific and positive enough? For example, 'I want to develop strong self-esteem', 'I want to be relaxed and in control', 'I want to be more assertive', 'I want to exude confidence'. Negative goals give you only what you do not want.

2. When you think about achieving your goal, can you experience it in every sense? Do you know how it will smell, taste, sound and look as well as feel? Think about that now. How do you feel about it? Unless you feel extremely good in every sense when thinking about what you want, it is unlikely you will spend much time on it.

3. How much control do you have? Who is standing in the way of a more confident you? Prepare yourself for any

obstacles you might encounter along the way. For example, people may put you down, so remind yourself that their opinion is just their opinion; it does not mean you are not a worthwhile person, or that they are necessarily right!

4. Do you have a plan? We can only climb mountains one step at a time. Think about the steps you will need to take in order to get closer to what you want. In order to make getting started easier and to help improve your motivation, break down your desired achievement into a series of mini-achievements. This will allow you to track and celebrate your progress as you move towards what you want, and give you the opportunity to make amendments or correct mistakes along the way.

5. Does it fit in with the rest of your life? If it doesn't, that will have to change too.

Once you are satisfied with the checklist above, think again about what you want. Write it down, say it out loud to yourself, picture yourself as already having achieved it. Then, sitting somewhere comfortably, with ample time at your disposal and perhaps playing your favourite music, answer the following questions.

1. What do I want, specifically?
2. When, where and with whom do I want it?
3. What will be different as a result of achieving this?
4. How will I know when I have got it?
5. What will achieving this do for me, get for me or give me?
6. How do I feel about it?
7. What resources do I need to achieve it?
8. What will I see, hear, feel, smell and taste once I have achieved it?
9. How will I look and sound once I have achieved it?
10. What will happen if I achieve this?
11. What won't happen if I achieve this?
12. What will happen if I don't achieve this?
13. What won't happen if I don't achieve this?
14. What would I be able to keep by not achieving this?
15. How do I know that what I want is worth having?
16. How will having it affect my life, my family, my job, my friends?

The answers will give you an idea of what needs to happen if you want to achieve what you want.

You control your future, your destiny. What you think about comes about. By recording your dreams and goals on paper, you set in motion the process of becoming the person you most want to be. Put your future in good hands – your own.

MARCH VICTOR HANSEN

Increase Your Motivation

Are you feeling 100 per cent motivated to change?

Motivation is really no more than persuading yourself to do whatever it is you want to do. We have all had some experience of being motivated; we simply have to learn how to put that feeling to work in the direction we want. To do this you have to make what you want to do so compelling, and what you no longer want to do so repellent, that you want to get on and do the new thing and abandon the old NOW.

On a scale of 1 to 100, your motivation to change is probably hovering between 70 and 80. You are thinking about change, and in doing so generating and strengthening the belief that you can change. How about we increase that motivation further towards your goal? Motivation is, after all, nothing more than a feeling about something, and it is just as easy and effective to motivate you away from your habits as it is to motivate you towards the new you.

Have you ever thought about the long-term consequences of continuing with your self-destructive behaviour?

Turn up the pain of not taking action so it gets you to the point that you think: I have got to do something about this.

Exercise – Generating Motivation to Change

You really need someone to read this exercise to you, or tape-record yourself reciting it. The first part is designed to get you to imagine what would happen if you did not change, and the second part helps you to see what life will be like once you have conquered your low self-esteem.

Part 1
1. Sit comfortably.
2. Think about your low self-esteem.
3. Close your eyes and do the exercise that gets you into a relaxed and controlled state (*, page 37).

There are risks and costs to a programme of action, but they are far less than the long-range risks and costs of comfortable inaction.

JOHN F. KENNEDY

4. Think now about what would happen if you do nothing whatsoever, but go on as you are now with this low self-esteem.

5. Imagine you still have low self-esteem in six weeks' time. Look in the mirror. Notice what you look like, sound like, smell like and feel like.

6. How do you feel about yourself? How do other people feel about you? What sort of things do you say to yourself?

7. Now take the feeling of discomfort you get from having carried on with your low self-esteem for another six weeks, and imagine yourself still like this in six months' time.

8. You have dragged with you into the future all the misery of having continued with your self-destructive behaviour, and arrive in front of another mirror.

9. Look at yourself. See what you look like, sound like, smell like and feel like. Look at your muscle tone and your complexion. Look at the expression in your eyes.

10. How do you feel about yourself now? What do you say about yourself? What are other people saying about you?

11. Now imagine you have continued with the behaviour you want to stop for a year. All that pain, all that discomfort is magnified by another 365 days, as you look once more into the mirror.

12. Have a good look at yourself. What do you smell, sound, look and feel like?

13. What do you say to yourself? What do other people say to you? How do you feel about yourself?

14. Take that feeling and project it another five years into the future, hauling with you all the associated discomfort.

15. Now see again what you look like, sound like and feel like. Do you like what you see? Do you like what you have become? How do you feel about yourself? What does the face you see tell you about that person?

16. Now take the consequences of having behaved in this way and think about what you will be like in another 10 years, should you still have low self-esteem.

17. Look at yourself in the mirror. Look at what you can see in that reflection and notice how you sound and feel, having continued to behave in that way for a decade. Do you like what you can see? Do other people like what they see? What do they say about you? What do you say about yourself?

18. Is that the person you want to be in 10 years' time?

Stop now for a moment.

Thank yourself.

None of this has happened.

Take a couple of deep breaths, and be grateful.

You can change what has not yet occurred.

That was only an imagined future. It could happen, but it does not have to.

You get what you focus on.

Are you 100 per cent motivated to change?

If you are not ready to change your behaviour, go back and do this exercise again and again and again, until you are. Imagining the consequences of not changing is often the quickest way to decide you want to change.

If that does not work, get someone else to do the exercise with you until you are convinced you want to stop your habit. Where it will take you is so repellent that you don't even want to think about having that habit any more.

If, on the other hand, you know you are ready to change after doing this exercise, take a short break: have something to drink or go for a walk.

Having taken a sufficient rest, take four or five deep breaths before moving on to the second part of this exercise.

It's time to turn up the pleasure of how much better you will feel once you have busted your habit of low self-esteem for good.

Every great and commanding movement in the annals of the world is the truimph of enthusiasm. Nothing great was ever achieved without it.

RALPH WALDO EMERSON

Part 2

1. Sit comfortably, feet flat on the floor, take a few deep breaths.
2. Do the state exercise*.
3. Now think about what you will look like in six weeks' time, having made the decision to change.
4. You have not had feelings of worthlessness nor put yourself down for 42 days. Look in the mirror.
5. Notice how you look, what you can hear and how it feels to be free from your low self-esteem.
6. Do you like what you see? What would you say to yourself? What do others say about you? What other changes have you made as a consequence of breaking your habit of low self-esteem?
7. Take all of that pleasure and go six months into the future.
8. Free from low self-esteem, you look in the mirror. Notice what you look like, sound like, smell like and feel like now you are in control and free. See how it feels to have more energy, excitement and passion.
9. What do you say to yourself? What do others say to you? How do you feel about yourself?
10. You have broken your habit of low self-esteem for a year now. Imagine arriving once again in front of a mirror.
11. Look at what you can see, hear and feel now that you are free.

12. What do you say to yourself? What are others saying about you? How do you feel now that you have felt positive about yourself for an entire year and have moved on? What other things might you be doing? How is your life different?

13. Imagine going five years into the future. You have not had low self-esteem for so long you can barely remember it. It is a distant memory.

14. You arrive in front of another mirror. Have a look at what you can see in the reflection, notice what you can hear and how it feels to be free and in control.

15. How do you feel about yourself? How do other people feel about you?

16. Now you are 10 years into the future, free from low self-esteem, and you see yourself in the mirror.

17. Once again, be aware of what you can see, hear and feel.

18. Listen to what you say about yourself, what others say about you, and notice how it feels to have been living for 10 years without low self-esteem. Notice how positive and powerful and in control you feel.

Now, slowly take a few deep breaths.

With each breath, breathe in that confidence you now feel. You should feel good: in control and relaxed.

Remember, you need to do these motivation exercises as many times as it takes to get you ready for change. For many people these exercises are often enough to get them to make the change. But if you are still not motivated to change, go back and do them again and again until you know that you are.

Desire is the key to motivation, but it's the determined commitment to an unrelenting pursuit of your goal, a commitment to excellence, that will enable you to attain the success you seek.

MICHAEL JORDAN

Believe That You CAN Change

step 8

This step is a very important one because until you can *truly* believe that you can change, you are going to find it very difficult to do so.

One of the brain's many functions is to confirm what we believe. What many people often do automatically is look out for anything that substantiates their ideas about themselves and the world. So if you believe something is possible, you will create the behaviour that supports this belief. Our brains are always actively engaged in perpetuating what is happening now. It happens automatically. You choose what is happening in your head, and your brain generates more of it.

If you expect building your self-esteem to be difficult, it probably will be. But when you believe you are capable of change and are actually changing, your attention is focused on this message, which reinforces the new, positive belief. Until you can believe you can break your self-destructive habits, you are going to find it very difficult to succeed, because belief and behaviour are intrinsically linked.

If you truly believe you can break your habit of low-self esteem, you act in ways that support the belief.

Exercise – Building a Powerful Belief

When you go to see a movie, particularly an action film, the director is trying to give you an experience through all of your senses. Much the same thing is happening with the following exercise: you are making up an experience that just happens to be true. As well as proving to you just how capable you are, we will also develop from this exercise an affirmation – a positive statement about yourself you know to be true, which will help you to achieve your goal.

You might find doing the second part of this exercise easier with your eyes closed and with someone else reading it out to you, or you could tape-record it yourself.

People are always blaming circumstances for what they are. I do not believe in circumstances. The people who get on in this world are the people who get up and look for the circumstances they want, and if they cannot find them, make them.

GEORGE BERNARD SHAW

Part 1

1. Get your notebook and, giving yourself plenty of time with perhaps some music playing in the background, write down as many instances as you can of times in your life when you:
   - performed well at a task
   - were praised for a task
   - persisted in the face of obstacles or difficulties
   - gave 100 per cent to some project
   - learned and mastered a new skill.

   It could be any moment, and the event could be or might seem to be trivial. One of my earliest memories of a moment of achievement is being able to tie my shoelaces, but it could be anything: the way you work, how you keep your house in order, what you do as a hobby, the way you dealt with a potentially self-damaging situation, the day you passed your driving test or bought a house or tiled the bathroom.

   Take time to recall and write down all the events you can remember. It does not matter if it takes a few days. Aim to have about 30 on your list.

2. When you have a nice long list, read them all through as though it were a list of achievements of someone you have never met.

3.   Now choose the five of which you are most proud. These are the ones that, when you think about them, give you the best feeling.

4.   Arrange them in your mind so one event can follow another (not necessarily in chronological order), almost like a movie or documentary of which you are the director.

Part 2

1.   Now, sit comfortably and get into state* (page 37).

2.   Imagine you are sitting in the cinema and are about to start watching a film in which you are starring. It is a film about those five experiences all put together.

3.   Watch the film on a big screen in front of you slowiy from beginning to end, taking particular note of how you perform in the starring role.

4.   Make what you are looking at bigger by doubling the size of the screen, and give the movie house surround sound.

5.   Notice how good it feels to watch yourself on this huge screen in full colour in those moments of achievement.

6.   As it ends, let the movie start over again so that it never actually finishes, and each time it begins the quality of the colour and sound become better and better and the film is brighter, sharper and clearer.

7. Scrutinize each event and notice how it feels, looks and sounds to watch that you on the big screen.
8. Think about how well that you has done, how much energy that you puts into each of those experiences.
9. As the film starts again, the picture is even larger and the volume is even greater. Repeat this at least five times.
10. Now stop.
11. Take a few deep breaths and bring your attention back to wherever you are.

Now do a critique: what would you say were among the qualities of the person you were watching? Would you give this person an Oscar for their performance? If not, go back and do it again, even if you have to go overboard and make up some of the situations.

Once they have given an award-winning performance, answer the following questions.

What would you say about this person? What are their qualities?
Are they persevering, no matter what?
Are they determined and focused on what they want?
Are they dedicated to self-improvement?
Are they really positive and filled with self-belief?

When the heart weeps for what it has lost, the spirit laughs for what it has found.

SUFI APHORISM

Write down the qualities you attribute to them. Make what you have written into a really powerful statement, such as 'They are really positive', 'They are very focused', 'They can do anything', 'They have got what it takes'.

Now I want you to get out of the director's chair and step into this Oscar-winning performance while repeating the statement. But instead of saying: 'They are really positive', say 'I am really positive', so your statement becomes a personal affirmation.

1. Now get back into state*.
2. Instead of sitting in the director's chair, step inside to take the lead role in your film and feel what it is like to experience those events all over again.
3. See what you saw, listen out for what you heard, and feel what it was like to achieve success in each instance.
4. Each time you go over this amazing feature-length film, feel how good it is in each of those events.
5. Repeat your affirmation to yourself, for example, 'I am always in control'. Say it as though you mean it, feeling the words inside your body as though you were shouting them from the rooftops.
6. Make the movie more real each time – brighter, bolder, clearer, louder – and go through it at least five times. It must be as though it never ends; it is just a continuous movie.

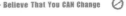

7.   Then take a few deeper breaths before slowly bringing your attention back to where you are.

If you are not convinced that you deserve an Oscar for that performance, do the exercise again. You can have as many takes as you like to perfect your performance and your realization that you have the power to change.

Once you know you can, think:

What was it about you then that helped you to succeed?
Were you motivated?
Were you confident?
Did you believe you could achieve?

Repeat the sentence you chose for yourself as the film critic: 'I persevere no matter what', or 'I am determined and focused on what I want'.

Say it aloud, with conviction, and mean it.

This is your affirmation. Repeat it to yourself at least 100 times a day, always like you mean it. Make a note now in your notebook of the affirmation, as we will be using it in the 'Power Moves' exercise in Step 11.

I would also like you to get into the habit of saying it to yourself whenever you feel your self-belief beginning to ebb, or when you want to be particularly effective or just more positive about your ability to achieve. It could be anything. Don't worry if it feels silly at first or you don't really believe it. Repeat it enough and you will. The more you use it, the better you will become at using it.

What you are doing is drawing on the resources you already have, which, in the past, helped you to achieve success. What you should have realized is that you are far more resourceful than you think.

Now that you have watched and starred in the movie a few times, how do you feel?

With that feeling, think of some of the challenges that lie ahead along the habit-breaking path. Do they seem like problems to the person whose achievements you have relived? You should be able to contemplate and face the challenges ahead with considerably more ease than before you sat down to make that list.

Mini Exercise – Repeat Your Affirmation, Over and Over Again

Write down your affirmation in colour on a few pieces of paper and stick them up in places where you will see them regularly each day. Whenever you see the affirmation, repeat it out loud to yourself a few times as though saying it from the top of a mountain or shouting it from the rooftops.

There is but one cause of human failure and that is man's lack of faith in his true Self.

WILLIAM JAMES

Play a Different Version of You

Have you noticed that some actors are so good at playing a role that you forget they are acting at all? Many of the best spend huge amounts of time getting into a part, thinking about how the character would think, feel, act and move through the world. As I mentioned earlier, we are not born with low self-esteem; we practise the behaviour, just like an actor learning a new role. All that I am trying to do now is to teach you how to break that habit and play a different version of you.

Simply imagining an event or great experience has an effect on the body. In an experiment conducted for a science-based television programme, a group of people were told to regularly imagine doing exercise. Although the difference was tiny, small muscle definition was detected a few weeks later, and all the control group had used to change their body shape was their minds.

Life can only be understood backwards; it has to be lived forwards.

SØREN KIERKEGAARD

This might sound crazy, even unbelievable, but if we think about it, the nervous system that connects the whole body starts in the brain, which sends messages to and collects messages from the rest of the body. It actually makes sense that what happens in one will have an effect in the other.

Research on sportsmen and -women using a biofeedback machine has also shown that as they imagine themselves competing, their heart rate, blood pressure and body temperature rise, as if they were actually competing physically. As this is the case, the potential for using our own imaginations in this way is enormous.

Before the 400-metre hurdles race in 1993 in which Sally Gunnell broke the world record, she spent months and months winning the race in her head. In minute detail she saw herself at the start-line, then setting off, running the race and then crossing the finish line first. She went over and over the experience in her head, time and time again, so that every time she imagined the race, it was as though she were actually there, running it. She later said, after breaking the world record, that for a minute or two after the race she had not been sure whether she really had won it or whether it had been in her imagination. So many times had she been over the race in her head in the months before the race, convincing herself she was going to win, that she could barely tell the difference between the real race and the imagined one.

Exercise – Making a Movie of Your Future

Remember that movie of your own success that you starred in in Step 8? We can make it into a blockbuster, with absolutely no expense spared. In the movie you have broken your habit. You are strong and in control. Some people find this difficult, but remember you are making this up. It lets you use your imagination. And if you don't get it right first time, you have the budget to make changes.

1. Get into state*.
2. Think of five scenarios in the future in which you are free from your habitual low self-esteem.
3. Imagine these five experiences as pictures or snapshots in front of you.
4. Take the first one and see it moving closer to you until it is big enough to fill a large screen.
5. Look at yourself in the future, free from low self-esteem, confident, positive and in control. Watch yourself carefully.
6. Make the picture clearer, brighter and bolder.

7. After 30 seconds, push the image back and repeat this process with each of the other four pictures.

8. Now, one at a time, allow each picture to move towards you until it moves inside you. Step into it for 30 seconds, feeling what it is like in the future to be in control and taking on the new way of behaving.

9. Do this with each snapshot, stepping in and out for 30 seconds, making sure each time that you make the experiences clearer and more real to you.

10. Finally, when you have done this with all the experiences, bring them all together and step into the entire event like it is an ongoing movie, with one future event following another. When it ends just start it again, making it even better. Keep going over it several times.

11. When you watch the film see yourself clearly, as though the future has already passed and you are watching a video recording. It must be as though the achievement has already happened, and there is nothing you can do about it. Your mind will then know the direction in which you want to go.

Doing this exercise once is rarely enough. You would not expect an actor to read a script through once to really get into the part. Go over and over it until you convince yourself you are that future you. Make it like Sally Gunnell so that when it comes to imagining these events, you feel as though you are already there. You can, if you think you can.

Imagine yourself in the future, free from low self-esteem, confident, positive and in control.

Mini Exercise – Ask Others How They Did It

Is there someone you have watched undergo a remarkable change? It might be losing weight, gaining confidence, changing career or just being happier. A friend of mine who began exercising underwent just such a change. His sour expression disappeared, his beer-belly started to shrink and he looked happier and more in control of his life. We all wanted to know how he had done it. If you know or ever meet anyone who tells or demonstrates a life-changing transformation, why not ask them how they did it? Their formula may not work the same wonders for you, but it would be worth a try.

The snow goose need not bathe to make itself white. Neither need you do anything but be yourself.

LAO-TSE

Make Up Memories

Many couples who are still together after more than 40 years say that to get through tough times they kept on looking for the good in each other, and never went to bed on an argument. Scientists now believe this timeless piece of advice ('Never go to bed on an argument') to have sound physiological grounding, for there is quite a lot of evidence to suggest that short-term memory takes quite a while to be encoded into long-term memory, and one of the processes that facilitates the transfer is sleep.

It is therefore possible to take control of what in the longer term you are most likely to remember. This is why children who have had potentially bad experiences with animals, such as falling off a horse, are encouraged as soon as possible to get back on and enjoy riding again. This prevents the memory of the fall becoming too ingrained, while allowing the enjoyment of being on the back of a horse to over-ride it.

One of the quickest and easiest ways to change a behaviour is to re-remember it.

When you re-remember an event or conversation or behaviour going the way you would have liked, you are setting a new direction for your life. Choose what you remember, excluding the bits that you wish hadn't been there, and you may find you behave differently next time.

Exercise – Re-remembering Past Behaviour

1. Get into state*.
2. Can you think of the last time you were irritated or cross about something, or ended a conversation feeling bitter or dissatisfied?
3. When you look back on it and retell the story of the event to yourself in your head, how do you feel?
4. Sometimes you can laugh at how you behaved, or think of how you might have handled the situation differently.
5. Think of the last time you lapsed in your continuing attempt to break your habit of low self-esteem.
6. Look back at yourself from the outside and watch yourself dealing with that situation.

7. What would you do differently if you were there now, standing by and watching yourself?
8. What if you could reach out as this other you, this other person, struggles, and tickle them under the chin?
9. What happens then?
10. How do they react?

This technique can be used to change the memory of having failed in the past, or immediately after a lapse as you try to break your habit of low self-esteem: the next time you are faced with a similar set of circumstances, your memory is not of giving in to the temptation, but of resisting it.

It's never too late to be what you might have been.

GEORGE ELIOT

Boost Your Confidence

What is confidence? Confidence is a feeling, just like any other feeling, but when we feel confident, we feel good about ourselves and in control. Feelings are just chemicals that are mixed inside our brain. People with low self-esteem generally lack confidence in themselves, so I want you to develop the habit of mixing your own cocktail of chemicals. Rather than automatically mixing those which induce feelings of being worried or stressed, you can learn to mix feelings of confidence or being relaxed or happy.

I find that many people need their confidence building up when trying to change their self-destructive behaviour. Those almost inevitable times of weakness that people experience can make them feel vulnerable, and as a result they can lapse back into their old ways. This is when they need to put themselves into a resourceful state, and rise above temptation. Many do this by repeating the affirmation they wrote down in Step 8 (see page 81), or by using some other exercise that helps restore their confidence.

What follows are some powerful techniques that you can turn to whenever you feel the need for extra confidence or self-control.

Exercise – Circles of Confidence

You may think other people are more talented, luckier or happier than you, and so naturally feel more confident. Maybe some of them do have a better match between inner resources and opportunities, but most successful people have learned to draw on the positive experiences in their lives to build stronger beliefs in themselves and their ability to achieve. They also draw from negative experiences, but only to learn from them before moving on.

I believe our basic quality of life, and therefore how we feel about ourselves, comes down to how we filter what happens to us. Think about some wonderful experiences from your own life and write them down. These can be times when you felt happy and confident and were having fun. What happens when you recall these times? Do you remember the experience as though it were happening now, or do you recall the memory from a distance, as though you were watching a replay on TV?

1.   Get into state*.
2.   Take one of those experiences now and imagine seeing it
     on a big screen.
3.   Make it bigger, brighter, bolder, clearer and imagine the
     picture starts moving closer to you till it moves inside you
     and you step back in and relive it.
4.   Repeat this with each of the positive experiences.

1.   Now think of a few difficult experiences in your life – no
     major issues, just times when you had to deal with
     adversity or apparent failure.
2.   What happens when you think about these times?
3.   Are you back there in the experience, or can you watch it
     from a distance?

Neither way of recalling an event is right or wrong – it is just the
difference in how we have filtered what has happened to us that
counts. We need to get some distance from the negative experiences, and move closer to the times we enjoy.

   Successful people have learned how to distance themselves
from uncomfortable experiences in their lives. Because they
have done this they have a great many positive experiences to
draw from, and accordingly think, act and expect positive
things to happen. Many of us do the opposite and find it hard to

recall happy times. We expect things to go wrong, like expecting to fail at breaking a habit.

1. Get into state*.
2. Imagine seeing yourself, as though on a television screen, in the negative experience.
3. Imagine the screen gets smaller, shrinks and moves further away.
4. Make the picture black and white and push it so far away that it is no bigger than the head of a pin.
5. Now make it disappear.
6. Think about the experience again, and notice the difference. It is difficult to feel the same way about it.
7. Do this as many times as you need to, to make the process automatic.

In being able to recall happy memories, it should be clear that you know how to feel confident. You also feel this way when doing something you are good at and/or enjoy. It could be cooking, ironing, playing tennis, doing karate or dancing. What you might not know is how to harness that feeling and use it as and when you want to. This is what the next exercise will teach you to do.

1. Make a list of all the times in your life when you had a really strong, confident feeling.
2. Pick five of the best and stand up, making sure you have some space in front of you.
3. Get into state*.
4. Imagine a coloured circle in front of you, big enough for you to step into.
5. Recall one of those confident experiences in your life.
6. Imagine you can see yourself in that experience inside the circle.
7. See what you look like, sound like and feel like, watching that you.
8. When you have a strong recollection of this and are ready, step into the circle and straight back into the experience as though you are there now.
9. Relive that feeling of confidence, making the experience more alive and colourful.
10. When you have absorbed as much confidence as possible from the memory, step out of the circle.
11. Repeat this exercise again with each of the other confident experiences in your life, using your imagination to allow each event to be better than the last as you keep adding to the confidence you already experience in the circle.

12. When you have done it with each experience, step into the circle and relive them again, one straight after the other.
13. Now, think of a time in the future when you will need those feelings of confidence.
14. Imagine yourself in the circle just before you need to be confident – in other words, just before you are usually triggered to fall back into your old habit.
15. As you see yourself, step into the circle and feel the confidence spreading right around your body.
16. Imagine the situation you foresee unfolding around you, with self-confidence fully available to you.
17. Step out of the circle and think about the difficult situation you face.
18. Notice how different you feel about it.

You can take this imaginary circle with you, or you could use the power of your imagination to turn the circle into a bracelet.

1. Look at the circle on the floor. Shrink it in your mind's eye.
2. Look at its bright and shiny colour.
3. Now pick it up and slip it onto your wrist.
4. Squeeze it around your wrist and, as you do so, allow the feelings of confidence that it gives off to spread throughout your body.

Whenever you need to feel confident in the future, especially before going into a situation you know might be a challenge, squeeze your imaginary bracelet, feel the confidence and deal with the situation.

In addition to this, when you experience times of feeling confident in the future, make your bracelet stronger by squeezing it and adding that feeling to it.

Distance yourself from the negative experiences in your life and move closer to the times you enjoy.

Exercise – Power Moves

Some time ago I was working with a former Olympian sports medallist who, minutes before we were due to stand up to do a presentation in front of 100 people, disappeared into the Gents saying he wanted to get himself ready. This for him meant standing in a semi-crouched position, his knees bent and one foot in front of the other, shouting at the top of his voice 'YES, YES, YES.' Others passing by outside might have wondered what was going on, but he did not care. All that concerned him was getting into the right state to give the best presentation he could.

Think of some of the professional sportspeople you might have watched on television. Many of them make what may sound to us like strange noises, or shout particular words as they hit a tennis ball or throw a football. They do this because, having practised over and over, they have come to know the result it will produce.

Recall the affirmation you wrote in the belief exercise in Step 8 (page 81).

Write it down again here: _____

_____

I am going to ask you to do the Future You exercise in Step 5 again (page 50).

This time, when you step into the future you I want you to repeat your affirmation to yourself, out loud or in your head, and at the same time do some physical movement to maximize the effect of this affirmation. Some people like to make a fist and punch the air, or draw their clenched fist back towards their waist as they would on having achieved a much sought-after goal. One friend of mine looks in the mirror, smiles, clenches his fist and says 'Go baby, go', while another does the Can Can! It need not be that dramatic, but with practice, it will work.

Find some sort of physical movement you can do as you recite your affirmation which reinforces the feeling of 'I can' – this can help you to get into a state ready for change.

Try doing it now: your own 'Power Move' should help you to feel the words in your affirmation throughout your body.

Doing this in a rather half-hearted way will not do. It needs to be done with conviction.

If the words 'Power Move' sound uncomfortable for you, call it your Success Signal, or even Dave.

1. Imagine standing outside your front door.
2. The door opens and you see yourself in the future, with high self-esteem.
3. You are feeling stronger, more powerful and in control.
4. Look at that you.
5. In a moment you are going to step into that you as though you were trying on how it feels.
6. As you step in, repeat the affirmation and do your Power Move or Success Signal.

DO IT NOW!

Once you have done this exercise a few times at home and are skilled at it, you can do it almost anywhere, though you don't have to say the affirmation out loud. Repetition enforces the message, so the more often you can do it, the better.

A consultant friend of mine told me that he always received many accolades at the end of his group sessions, but tended to brush them off. Then one day he decided that those who complimented him must have good reason, and were probably not in the habit of lying, so he began looking in the mirror before he left for work each day playing back to his reflection some of the compliments he regularly received.

By living out the person he was told he was, his work got better, as did the commendations. When one woman once remarked on how attractive he was, he repeated the technique and within weeks dozens more women were making comments on his appearance. Believing that other people believed these things about him helped this consultant to behave as they were expecting, but to an even greater and more demonstrative extent.

From now, instead of criticizing yourself, get into the much more useful habit of beginning and ending your day by looking in the mirror and repeating your affirmation with or without your Power Move. Do it whenever you see your reflection or when you need to motivate yourself for a particular task. See what sort of a difference it makes, both to your behaviour and your attitude towards and about yourself.

You are the only one who can give yourself self-confidence.

Exercise – Re-centring Your Balance (Hara)

When asked, a friend of mine said the best thing about practising martial arts was the ability and confidence it gave him to say 'no'. It gave him control of himself and the state he was in, to the point where he could not be swayed by any outside influence. In practising this discipline, he was able to go into this state whenever he wanted or needed to.

Many practised martial artists are able to go into whichever state they want whenever they want. I once saw a show given by some martial artist monks who were demonstrating strength and flexibility by lying on beds of nails and doing somersaults in the air. These are people who have learned how to put their attention into the strongest part of their body: their centre.

Imagine you have a small tennis-size ball in the middle of your stomach, the strongest point in your body. Breathe into that part of your body and feel strong.

Whom do you know or admire who can stay in a resourceful state no matter what? When we are in a negative state of mind, we talk down to ourselves and our attention is all in our head. When we feel good, confident and strong, our attention is more evenly spread through our body and tends to concentrate in our centre, our stomach, making us feel much more balanced. Could you imagine the golfer Tiger Woods or the former South African President Nelson Mandela talking to themselves negatively or giving themselves a hard time when under pressure?

Get a friend to stand by you for this next exercise.

1. Stand straight up with your eyes on the horizon and your feet shoulder-width apart.
2. Now think of a time when you've felt overwhelmed or stressed, perhaps at the amount of work in front of you, or at a task you've had to complete by a particular time.
3. You no doubt felt anxious and concerned about how you were going to get through this time.
4. As you concentrate on this feeling of anxiety and stress, tell your friend to push against your upper arm just below the shoulder in an attempt to force you over.
5. You should find that you are unable to put up much resistance: your brain is too focused on your problems to divert any strength to keeping you upright.

6. Now, find the point on your lower stomach which is about
    three finger-width spaces below your belly-button. This is
    called *hara* by those who practise yoga. Press a finger on
    that point and, as you take your finger away, relax
    completely and put your attention on that point.
7. Get your friend to try to push you over again. You should
    find that, this time, you are much more solid.

We spend much of our time with our attention fixed in our heads,
worrying mostly, and wonder why we often feel wobbly and out
of control.

When you need to feel more stable or in control, just switch
your focus from your mind to that point below your naval. Your
ability to face whatever difficulty you confront will automatically
increase.

**Fate somehow ensures that certain events
come to pass; how they are handled it leaves up
to you.**

The more you depend on forces outside yourself, the more they dominate you.

HAROLD SHERMAN

Start Taking Care of Yourself

Step 12

I have learned that success in breaking a habit does not last if I give people the skills and techniques without also offering them something to replace the habit with. We all need to take on a different habit and commit to doing something else.

The habit of a lifetime, for most of us, should be taking care of ourselves. But the majority of people, for a number of different reasons, do not know how to do this. Mainly it is because of the ways in which we have been conditioned as we have grown up, so that often the biggest habit any one of us has is not taking care of ourselves.

Some years ago I was suffering from exhaustion and needed to take some time off work. But I was self-employed, so I didn't. I suffered for the following four years, constantly having to take time off without ever properly recovering. Being that unwell for so long was tough, but it taught me one of the most important lessons I think I will ever learn. I had been doing what I wanted, rather than what I needed, to do. I wanted to go on working regardless, but I needed to have more fun, space, time on my own and recreation to recharge my batteries. I had forgotten how to take care of myself and knew only how to take care of others. Of course, I had let myself get into a situation where I could not take care of anyone, let alone myself. Over time I learned that the best way to help others was to help myself.

One of the questions that I really enjoy asking people is what they think they will wish they had done less of once they reach the age of 90. Most commonly the responses are 'I wish I'd worried less' or 'I wish I had not been so negative'.

Ask yourself this question, then write the answers down in your notebook.

I always follow this question with another. When you are 90, what do you think you will wish you had done more of? People often say laughed more, travelled more or had more fun.

Answer this question yourself, writing the answer in your notebook.

You are (probably) not 90. Many people, having done this exercise, find this a huge relief. It makes them realize that the way they are now, the way they think and the things that they

There is only one success – to be able to spend your life in your own way.

CHRISTOPHER MORELY

do are not set in stone. It is possible to change, if they really want to.

You could quite easily now say 'Oh, well, I will change tomorrow', or 'I will wait until things in my life calm down'. But life is always full of unforeseen circumstances. There will always be other people and events trying to grab your attention. You cannot wait for the perfect time – you have to work with what you have got. Putting things off and talking yourself out of change has already robbed you of so many opportunities. You don't have to repeat that mistake.

What follows are some simple techniques designed to help you start taking good care of yourself, today.

Take on board the habit of a lifetime – the habit of truly taking care of yourself.

Make Mistakes and Enjoy the Struggle

You are always going to have times of struggle; that is just a part of life. But it is your ability to deal with the struggle that matters. When you know you are struggling, change your attitude towards it and say to yourself 'I am going to enjoy this, because I will learn something from it and I know it will not last.'

I have found that the people who get on in life and are happy are the ones who have learned from whatever happens to them. They accept that adversity and struggle are an integral part of life, and that how they handle it will make the difference between staying behind or getting ahead.

Even though we often fail to realize it, some of the most important lessons we learn are through making mistakes, and the same principle applies when we make mistakes or have set-backs when trying to change our behaviour. If you do lapse, it does not mean you have to abandon your attempts at trying to change. Learn from it and move on. If you don't, it is likely you will repeat the mistake until you do. Keep changing your responses to your mistakes and you can change your life.

Be Successful at Being Happy

What does being successful mean to you? When asked, a great many people will define success as being when they have achieved something or reached a particular goal. Strange, what about all the times in between? You are being successful even on the way to achieving a goal. Start being successful at being happy, and judge your success by how happy you are.

The single stupidest sentence ever in the history of the English language is 'Do it right first time.' Nobody ever did anything even half interesting the 41st time.

TOM PETER

One of the secrets to doing this successfully is to love what you do and do what you love. I know this is not always easy, especially if you are in a job that you don't like or in a difficult relationship. But make a decision to enjoy what you do now, in the present, because that is what it is, a present, and it won't come round again. You are making your future now, so make the most of it.

Love what you do and do what you love.

Imagine a Better You

Imagine what it is going to be like once you are taking better care of yourself.

Grab your notebook and write down:

- what you would be doing
- what would be different about your life
- what you would be eating
- what kind of exercise you would be taking
- how often and in what way you would be relaxing
- what you would not be doing any more
- how you would be feeling.

See yourself behaving in these ways, as though you are already taking better care of yourself. You can then begin to live the dream. It really is no more difficult than that. Achieve little bits at a time, for as long as it takes. You can win in every step you take towards being kinder to yourself – and don't let anyone else, for whatever reason, pull you away from your purpose.

Nourish Yourself

What is the most powerful force on the planet? Love.

To take care of yourself, you need to nourish yourself, and nourishment can take many different forms. First, I believe, nourishment comes through love. It is the most powerful force on Earth, even though science cannot prove that it exists. Comfort is another dimension of nourishment, whether it be physical, emotional or mental. And so, of course, is diet.

Other sources of nourishment are the elements: the water we drink, the air we breathe, heat from the sun and the many foods we eat that owe their existence to being grown in the earth. Without any of these elements, we would be dead. The elements make life the way it is. Many of us forget what a wonderful world this is and what a great chance life can be.

Whatever you can do. Or dream you can. Begin it. Boldness has genius, power and magic in it. Begin it now.

GOETHE

I would urge you to get outside whenever you can to appreciate the most basic things in life such as a sunset or a river flowing or wind blowing through the trees. Enjoying peace and space is nourishment. We are so bombarded with information about how we should be or how we should think that we don't have time for either.

Most people try to satisfy a need for nourishment externally: by drinking, smoking, eating and so on. But the best possible sensation of nourishment you can give yourself is by learning to feel good. If you can get to the point at which you don't really need any sort of stimulus to feel good, you will appreciate compliments, love, gifts – or anything else that gives you that feel-good factor – that much more.

You may still think you're unworthy of any sort of happiness, success or nourishment – and perhaps to a certain extent you are right, because you have convinced yourself that this is the way you are. But it doesn't have to be that way. Whatever has happened to you in the past need not cloud or colour your future. Your life can change, and it can change for the better.

Enjoy Each Moment

We seem to live life at an incredibly high speed, trying to cram all that we believe we need to do into a day. This is despite using any number of devices to help us save time and get on with what needs to be done. What do people really do with the time they save? No time is saved, really; it just tends to get filled up with more 'doing'. There is still no time for stillness, for enjoying each moment.

Babies are brilliant at this. They do not mope for hours because their favourite toy was taken away, or worry and stress about where their next meal is coming from. As soon as an unpleasant event is over, they forget about it and they never fret about what might happen tomorrow. Most of us could do with relearning this and spend some time slowing down, relaxing, recharging our batteries and being in the present moment.

Some of the most priceless memories people have come from experiencing such oneness with a moment. Can you remember any such examples? The moment at a wedding when the smiling bride walks down the aisle; seeing a beautiful painting for the first time; being gripped by the cliff-hanger in a film or a book; or being with close friends on a once-in-a-lifetime holiday. The common thread running through all such examples is our being in the moment and not thinking about anything else, talking to ourselves or giving ourselves a hard time.

Mini Exercise – Time Out

When you are feeling particularly tired or stressed, perhaps during the course of a working day, stop whatever it is you are doing – this need take no longer than a minute. Either seated or standing, close your eyes. Straighten your back, keep your head erect, and relax your shoulders. Think of the thing you want most in the world. Picture yourself doing or having it – as though it has happened. Make the picture and feeling as real as you possibly can. Take a few deep breaths, open your eyes, and return to whatever you are doing in a more relaxed, happier and effective state of mind.

Be Grateful For What You Have

Start being aware of what you do have in life, and focus on the things you can be grateful for, for example, a home, healthy children, a job, friends and family. Like passion and love, gratitude is a powerful emotion. Think about a time when you were really grateful for something. Would you agree that it is a feeling that fills you up? Be grateful for each day. See it as a gift.

Exercise – Filling Yourself Up With Powerful Emotion

1. Take a few deep breaths.
2. Get comfy and, if it feels easier, close your eyes.
3. Think of all the things in your life you can be truly grateful for. You have two arms and legs, a home, healthy children, a job. You can feel grateful for places visited, for friends and family.
4. Relive the experiences or focus on the things you are grateful for having.
5. Imagine yourself filling up with all the gratitude you have.
6. Now think of all the things you feel passionate about. Doing the best for your children and friends, hobbies or other recreational pastimes, being involved with good causes or doing your job well.
7. Go through and relive all these things.
8. Imagine yourself filling up with all that passion and add it on top of the gratitude.
9. Think now about all the things you love – friends, parents, pets, music, art, poetry, sport, and so on.
10. See all these things, hear and feel them as you add the love to the passion and gratitude you feel and completely fill yourself up with these emotions all the way down to your toes, up to your nose and down to both hands.

11. Having filled yourself up with these emotions, take a few deep breaths and bring your attention back into the room. Open your eyes and feel alert and full of gratitude, passion and love.

You don't get to choose how you're going to die. Or when. You can only decide how you're going to live. Now.

JOAN BAEZ

A Final Word

Having read this book and completed some of the exercises, you might feel inspired and enlightened, and hopefully you had a good laugh, but are you going to change? It is very easy to think 'Yes, that was an interesting book' and then go back to the way you were before.

It doesn't matter how many self-development books you read, they won't make any difference at all unless you do something with them. They are just words on the page unless you choose to change and are prepared to take the action necessary to achieve it. Remember, it is your choices that make it possible to break habits.

Have you ever looked at people who are genuinely happy and wondered how they do it? What is their secret? Believe it or not, they are choosing to feel good about themselves. You, too, can choose to feel good about yourself.

It is time for you to take responsibility for your self-esteem – low self-esteem is a choice that you are making, but isn't high self-esteem a better choice to make? I promise you, it is a choice well worth making.

Good luck and take care of yourself, because you deserve it!

Follow your bliss.

JOSEPH CAMPBELL

Further Help

To find out more about Habit-busting, or if you are interested in working with one of our Habit-busters, please visit our website at:

www.Habitbusting.com

or email at:

info@Habitbusting.com

You can also write to us at:

Habit Busting
PO Box 2837
Leamington Spa
CV31 1WT

Tel: 0845 602 1607

Habit Busting

A 10-Step Plan That Will Change Your Life
Pete Cohen, With Sten Cummins

Simple Techniques to Stop Self-Sabotage, Break Bad Habits, and Achieve Your Potential

How would you like to be your best self all the time? To be free and successful at work? To eat healthily? To give up smoking? To stop procrastinating? According to the authors of *Habit Busting* it can be simple, it can be quick, and it can be fun.

In this invaluable guide Pete Cohen and Sten Cummins offer techniques to stop sabotaging yourself and straightforward strategies for bringing out your best. They will help you work with your strengths, learn from masters in whatever it is you want to accomplish and take stock of past behaviour – both what has worked for you and what hasn't. *Habit Busting* shows how, in just 21 days, you can turn a bad habit into a healthy one.

ISBN 0722540094

Fear Busting

A 10-Step Plan That Will Change Your Life
Pete Cohen

Following the success of his best-selling book *Habit Busting*, GMTV life coach Pete Cohen explains how to tackle the fears that prevent us from living the life we want, focussing on the fear of change.

- ⊘ Do you worry about making mistakes?
- ⊘ Are you afraid to try in case you get it wrong?
- ⊘ Is the fear of change making you make do with the life you have, when you know it could be so much better?

It doesn't have to be this way. In *Fear Busting*, Pete Cohen outlines simple strategies for tackling the fears that hold you back – especially the fear of change itself. By following Pete's motivational plan, you can change the way you see your life, so that challenges become chances, threats become opportunities and no obstacle is insurmountable.

ISBN 0 00 715109 8

Make
www.thorsonselement.com
your online sanctuary

Get online information, inspiration and
guidance to help you on the path to physical
and spiritual well-being. Drawing on the integrity
and vision of our authors and titles, and with
health advice, articles, astrology, tarot, a
meditation zone, author interviews and events
listings, www.thorsonselement.com is a great
alternative to help create space and peace
in our lives.

So if you've always wondered about practising
yoga, following an allergy-free diet, using the
tarot or getting a life coach, we can point you
in the right direction.